# The Bully Vaccine

# The Bully Vaccine

How to inoculate yourself against bullies
and other petty people

by Jennifer Hancock

Cover art by Nichol Cox

Published 2012


the United States of America
Text copyright 2012 by Jennifer Hancock

ISBN-13: 978-1475009910
ISBN-10: 1475009917

~~~~~~

Other books by Jennifer Hancock

*The Humanist Approach to Happiness: Practical Wisdom*
*Jen Hancock's Handy Humanism Handbook*


Other products available

*The Humanist Approach to Happiness Life Skills Course:*
*Living Made Simpler*


Learn more at:
http://www.jen-hancock.com

*I want to thank my friend Lisa Fite, who I have never met in person, but who insisted that I write this book next. Without her, this book would still be on the backburner.*

*I also want to thank my mom for teaching me how to be fearless and how to deal with bullies so that they left me alone.*

*I want to thank my friends from the Kewalo Basin Marine Mammal Laboratory. You all know who you are. Without you, I would have never learned how to train, or how to apply training principles to humans.*

*And finally, I want to thank my son, who has used these techniques himself and verified that they do indeed work and who is becoming more fearless every day. I love you and am proud of you.*

# Table of Contents

# Bullying in the Real World

*"The bullying was hideous and relentless, and we turned it round by making ourselves celebrities."*

- Julian Clary, gay British celebrity

With about seven billion people and growing, the planet becomes more crowded every day. Most of us are the *go along to get along* type who try to be nice to everyone we meet. There is, however, a small portion who are, simply put, obnoxious.

They may be petty, rude or just downright mean. It seems that wherever you go, there will be at least one obnoxious person, or perhaps a group of them, who will try to make your life miserable.

It's an almost certainty that at some point you will have to deal with bullies and/or petty and obnoxious people. So it's a good idea to be prepared and have a strategy to deal with these jerks before you encounter them.

## *Why This Book?*

This book is designed to act as a vaccine against bullies, jerks, and other obnoxious people.

By preparing for them in advance, you can effectively inoculate yourself against the worst of their behavior. Yes, they will still be obnoxious, but you won't be as annoyed and upset by their behavior and that is at least something.

The added benefit is that the less you are annoyed or upset by them, the less entertaining and satisfying a target you will be for them. Bullies and other jerks really do want an audience. The more you are able to not respond to their obnoxious behavior, the more quickly they will go look for someone else to annoy.

In this book I hope to:

- Help you understand what motivates bullies to behave the way they do.

- Help you understand that a bully's behavior toward you has absolutely nothing to do with you; even though the bully want you to believe it does

- Help you feel sorry for how miserable the bully really is (Even jerks deserve our compassion)

- Help you learn some basic coping techniques

- Finally, I hope to help you become fearless in the face of the truly obnoxious.

## *What is Bullying?*

According to Wikipedia, bullying is a form of aggressive behavior, which may manifest as abusive treatment. Bullying can be verbal, non-verbal or physical. While bullying can be defined in many different ways it is often directed persistently towards particular victims, because of race, religion, gender, sexuality, or ability.

The problem is that the word we use to describe bullying doesn't do the actual experience justice. When bullying involves hitting, kicking, punching and threatening, it is actually a form of criminal behavior and should be treated as criminal. But even if all that occurs is some name-calling, bullying is still abusive.

We should not ignore the emotional effects of bullying because they can be severe. Some victims suffer long-term stress problems as a result of bullying. Some people are so upset by the experience; they commit suicide to get away from the torment. Others have been known to retaliate by shooting their classmates. The better prepared you are to deal with it, the less you will suffer from its effects. Knowledge really is power.

## *What You Need to Know*

In any given bullying situation there are three types of people. The bully, the victim, and the bystanders who witness it.

## The Bullies

The reason bullies bully is because it works. It helps them achieve power and status that they would otherwise not be able to get on merit alone. Bullies get their power by making people afraid of them. We will get into why they do this later.

To make people afraid, bullies target people who are not able to properly defend themselves. They rarely target people who will stand up to them because if everyone found out the bullies could be stood up to, bullies would lose their power. This is why they target younger kids, disabled individuals, and anyone they can label as different.

## The Victims

As for the victims, pretty much everyone who isn't a bully is worried that at some point they will become a victim. Studies on bullying[1] estimate that 70 percent of kids are bullied in school at some point. It is an extremely common problem.

The good news is that while obnoxious people are inevitable, becoming their victims and allowing them to bully others is not. It can be stopped. But it takes courage, intelligence and a willingness to act, from both the victims and bystanders.

---

[1]  American Psychological Association – Bullying - http://www.apa.org/education/k12/bullying.aspx#

## The Power of the Bystanders

Bullies choose their targets carefully. They bully when they think no one is looking, or when they have allies on their side. They are hoping bystanders will ignore their actions and not report them. For this reason, bystanders have a very important role to play in the culture of bullying. Bystanders have the power to stop the bullies.

Bystanders generally fall into three distinct groups. A few have the courage to defend the victim. Most will do nothing in the hope that they won't become the next victim. And some will actively assist the bully to "get in good" hoping to get on the bully's good side.

The problem is bullies get their power by making other people afraid. The key to not being a bully's next victim is to take away their power by not being afraid of them.

This is easier said than done. After all, it is obvious that bullies tend to go ballistic whenever anyone dares to stand up to them. As a result, most bystanders do nothing. They are afraid and don't want to draw the bully's attention onto themselves.

Not doing anything does not work. Judging by the number of people who are bullied (nearly 70% at some point in their school career), not speaking up to defend a victim will not only fail to prevent a bully from turning on you, it will actually encourage them to bully more.

The other problem with not speaking up and defending a victim is that it makes it seem as if everyone agrees with the bully. The reality couldn't be further from the truth. Most bystanders are simply too afraid to speak up because the bully is so effective at enforcing silence through fear.

Bullies work hard to prevent people from coming to the defense of a victim by attacking anyone who dares to challenge them. But if you and a group of your friends gather up the courage to stand up to the bullies and come to the defense of their victims, and if you do that every single time a bully tries to bully someone, the bullying will stop. Permanently.

How does one stand up to a bully? By telling them what they are doing isn't OK. You don't need to fight them. You don't need to call them names. You simply need to say something like, "That isn't nice. You should apologize." That is all that is required. It puts the bully on notice that what they are doing isn't OK and let's everyone else know that you have the victim's back. If you witness someone being hurt, tripped, punched or harmed, report what you saw to a teacher and encourage the victim to report it as well. Bullying only works when people remain silent. Don't remain silent. Speak up.

The following chapters will provide you with the information you need to control your fears so that you can stand up to the bullies and confront them in an effective way. You have more power than you realize. You just need to gain the courage to wield it to defend the defenseless as well as yourself.

# Vaccinating Yourself Against Bullies

*"You cannot escape the responsibility of tomorrow by evading it today."*

- Abraham Lincoln

Most attempts to deal with bullying try to convince the bullies to stop doing what they are doing. These approaches don't work. The reason they don't work is because bullying works for the bully. They are getting a payoff for their bad behavior. Asking them nicely to stop isn't going to make that happen. The only way to get them to quit is to stop giving them the payoff they are looking for. The only way to do that is to no longer respond to them in fear. To do that, you need to strengthen your moral, mental, and emotional defenses against them. In other words, you need to vaccinate your mind to build up the defenses you need to stand up to them.

The best way to inoculate yourself against a bully is not to be the sort of person a bully likes to target. The best way to not become their target is to understand what makes bullies tick, what they fear and how to respond to them when (not if) they test you to see if you'd make a good victim.

### In an Ideal World

I realize that in an ideal world you wouldn't have to deal with this at all. And you shouldn't have to deal with it. No one should. But we don't live in an ideal world. We live in the real world and in the real world there are obnoxious jerks and bullies.

Sticking your head in the sand and hoping it will all go away doesn't work. Even if you manage to avoid becoming a target, others aren't going to be so lucky. It is far better to stand up to bullies than to live in fear of them.

Living in fear is very stressful. When there is a bully loose on the playground, everyone suffers from the stress that comes with worrying about who will be their next target. Trust me. If you are afraid of them, so is everyone else.

To inoculate yourself and others, you need to make a choice. Are you going to continue to allow bullies to control you by fear? Or are you going to take control over your life by refusing to play the game bullies are playing. And yes, this does take courage. And yes, you will have to stand up and defend yourself and others.

But what is your alternative? You can either allow bullies to control you and everyone else through fear or you can stand up to them and end it. Having been there and done that I have to say that standing up isn't nearly as scary as it seems and it is well worth the effort. You will be rewarded, both in terms of how much better your life is when you are not living in fear and in how much better you will feel about yourself for having had the courage to stand up to a bully.

### What My Mom Taught Me

The techniques I'm going to teach you, I learned from my mom. When I was first bullied, my mom taught me how to deal with bullies. Her technique was so effective that I not only never had to deal with being bullied again; some of my friends in high school nicknamed me "fearless leader" - a nickname I only learned about as an adult.

This technique works for most bullying and harassment situations. I realize you are going to doubt this actually will work. I know I was skeptical when my mom first taught it to me. But it worked and has continued to work for me throughout my life. The reason I wrote this book is to share her knowledge because it pains me to watch people suffer at the hands of bullies.

And don't think I had it easy. I didn't. I was physically deformed because I had a severe under bite. My lower jaw was basically huge. I was quite shy because of how I felt I looked. I was also a complete and total dork. In short, I was a perfect target for a bully.

Not only was I not bullied thanks to the advice my mom gave me, I gained so much confidence in myself that I actually ended up coming out of my shell. I was still a bit insecure about my jaw and there were still people who tried to put me down, but I didn't let them bother me or prevent me from doing the things I wanted to do.

By the time I got to high school, I became a bit of a social butterfly. I was elected drum major for the high school band at the end of my freshman year. In other words, despite my deformed face, I won a popularity contest and was elected to run the marching band, an honor usually reserved for seniors. I was able to make great friends who I still love and adore to this day for all their support. When you think about it: that's not too shabby for a shy girl who grew up with a deformed jaw.

So what is this amazing advice my mom gave me? Well, I'm glad you asked.

## The World Doesn't Revolve Around You

The first thing she taught me was that it really wasn't about me at all. I know it seems like it is all about you because you are being targeted and you are the one being affected But the reality is, you weren't targeted because of something you did or didn't do, so don't take what the bully is doing personally.

When it comes to bullies and other jerks, you need to realize that their behavior has everything to do with them and their fears and their insecurities. It would be sad if it weren't so obnoxious. Many people bully as a way to hide their own fears. They are afraid if they don't bully you, you will bully them.

Why is this knowledge important? Well, it turns out that when you understand that a bully isn't targeting you because of something you did or didn't do, they are targeting you out of their own fear and insecurity; it is soooooo much easier to no longer respond to them. Because it isn't about you. It is about them being too afraid and insecure to behave properly. You are just an easy target for their anger. It could have been anyone and everyone and it usually is.

The next time a bully says something mean to you, just remember: the world doesn't revolve around you. What they just said or did isn't about you. It is about them and their problems and their fears, which are so overwhelming, they don't know how to cope.

(To explore this concept and its various practical applications further, I recommend my other book, *The Humanist Approach to Happiness: Practical Wisdom,* which devotes an entire chapter to the world not revolving around you.)

### What Makes a Bully Tick?

Bullies do what they do because it works. Regardless of their reasons, bullies gain power by making other people afraid. This is why they rarely pick on people who are older or have higher status than them. They also don't pick on kids who don't respond the way they want. They are looking for people who they can scare. And that's the key to making yourself less attractive to them.

Clearly you can't do anything about your size or your age or any of the other reasons people get targeted by bullies. You are who you are. Only a few select people in any school are going to be popular. So don't count on that to save you either. This means you have only one good option: do not respond the way a bully wants you to respond.

What are bullies looking for? Bullies want people who are afraid of them, someone they can scare. It is like playing a video game. You press a button and something cool happens. That's basically what bullies are doing. They are pressing your buttons and the more you respond with fear, tears, or anger, the more they are going to want to bully you. It's as simple as that.

The less you respond with fear, tears, or anger the less interesting you are to them. The more you can face the taunts and threats and appear bored and uninterested, the less they will want to bully you. They are looking for someone who will be afraid of them.

## It All Comes Down to Fear

Most bullies are bluffing. Their bravado and threats are designed to make you afraid of them. The more afraid you are, the more power they have over you. It is a sick and sad game they are playing.

When I was in middle school, the biggest bully in the school was a kid named Greg. It turned out he was also one of the smartest kids in our school. But you wouldn't have known that by how he acted. He spent most of his time hiding the fact he was smart and the rest of his time trying to harass the smart kids for being smart. But one day, he just couldn't help himself. We had a spelling bee and Greg won. He beat out all the smart kids. His bullying was an attempt to hide the fact that he was a full-fledged geek. In other words, he was a dork and didn't want anyone to know it so he hid his geek-level smarts behind his bullying.

The motivation for many bullies is that they are afraid that you and your classmates are going to find out just how much of a dork they really are. These bullies bully to draw attention away from their own dorkiness onto someone who is dorkier.

It is a lot easier to not be afraid of someone when you understand just how much of a dork they really are.

# What a Dork

*"I think I've been able to fool a lot of people because I know I'm a dork. I'm a geek."*

- Gwen Stefani

Everyone knows that the dorkier you are, the more you are going to be teased and bullied. So everyone tries not to be a dork. The problem is, we are all dorks. We can't help ourselves. It is part of being human.

What the bullies don't want you to know is that they are also dorks. They try to hide it by being tough and picking on kids dorkier than them. But all they are trying to do is draw attention away from themselves onto others.

After all, if they are making fun of someone for being a dork, they must be cool? Right? Wrong! The people who make the most fuss about being cool are the most insecure and therefore the least cool. Being cool is all about not caring what other people think. If you care deeply about what other people think, you aren't cool. It is as simple as that.

Regardless, as soon as a bully starts picking on someone, just remember what a dork the bully really is. The fact that they are bullying someone is all the proof you need.

## *Embracing Your Inner Dork*

This may seem strange, but the really cool people in the world have all made peace with the fact that they are dorks. Think of your favorite actors, musicians and artists. They are all dorks. And they know it. They aren't afraid to be themselves, regardless of what other people think. They are OK with being different. In fact, that's probably why you like them. And that's what makes them cool.

You don't become cool by trying to live up to someone else's expectations of you. You become cool by no longer trying to fit in.

The great thing about embracing your inner dork is that it takes all the stress off of you. Once you stop trying to fit in, you can relax and be yourself. So what if someone calls you a dork. You are – 'nuff said. Teasing simply doesn't work on someone who has embraced the fact they are a dork and they are different.

It also frees you up to really enjoy the things you like. Even if what you really enjoy is classical music and you dream of being an opera singer someday, you don't need to hide that from your friends. Not everyone has those talents or dreams and it is pretty darned cool if you do. So embrace that about yourself and pursue the things that truly interest you.

The point is, when you accept and embrace whatever it is that makes you different, you inoculate yourself against the bullies because they can't make you feel ashamed of something you aren't ashamed of.

If what you are ashamed of is your looks, don't be. I have been there and done that. Most of my friends and family don't even remember that I had a deformed jaw growing up because they weren't paying attention to what I looked like. They were responding to my personality and the things I was doing and was interested in. In other words, people liked me because of who I was, not because of how I looked. In middle school I was a major dork who was completely obsessed with the Beatles and I wore a hoodie every day. My friends must have liked that. My strange looks only helped them to find me in a crowd.

At the end of the day, people will like you if you are a nice person. They won't if you aren't. Your looks have nothing to do with it.

In any school, there is a group of kids for whom how they look matters greatly. They try to tease people who don't look or dress like them. If you get to know some of these fashionistas you will quickly find that they aren't very nice and they spend an amazing amount of time worrying about how they look. That's their problem. Don't let them con you into thinking that you need to look a certain way to be cool. You don't. You just need to be a nice person who is interesting to be around.

## *Feeling Sorry For the Bully*

This brings us to the reasons why you should feel sorry for bullies. Their entire lives are built around the power games they are playing. Instead of trying to be a good person they give in to their fearful and/or aggressive impulses. To make them feel less alone and less afraid they do their best to make other people as scared as they are. For these bullies, whatever it is they are most afraid of in the behavior of others is often the thing they are most afraid of in themselves.

If a person bullies and teases other people about their looks, it is often because they are afraid about theirs. If they are bullying people for being smart, it is often because either they aren't and are jealous, or because they are, but they don't want people to know. If they are bullying someone who isn't cool, it is usually because they themselves are afraid that they aren't cool either. And finally, if someone is bullying people who are gay or who they think might be gay, it is often because they are afraid that they might be gay. They are hoping that by doing some gay bashing, no one will suspect them. And yes, studies do back this up![2]

The point is that being a bully means being unhappy and angry pretty much all the time. It is a very sad way to approach life. You should feel sorry for them.

This doesn't excuse their behavior. Everyone at some point feels scared. We all want friends and we all want to be liked. We all want to fit in and to get along with other people. That is normal. However, most of us don't become mean as a result. We just deal with it.

The problem for the bullies is that their worries and fears are too much for them to cope with. They simply aren't confident enough in who they are to trust that people will like them. So, they lash out to give people a good reason why they shouldn't like them. It sounds stupid, and it is, but that is what is going on.

---

[2] Adams, Wright and Lohr https://my.psychologytoday.com/files/u47/Henry_et_al.pdf - caution - this is explicit) A variety of additional studies have confirmed these findings.

23

The basic thinking of a bully is this: since people aren't going to like me anyway, I might as well make them afraid of me. This prevents them from making and having good friends. And again, that's pretty sad. Yes, they often have a small group of people who hang out with them and support them. These "friends" are often called henchmen. They ally with the bully out of fear and egg them on, giving them their support. The henchman strategy is to "friend" the bully so they won't become a target. However, this is a friendship based on fear and the bully often plays his or her henchmen off each other so all are vying for favored status. Kind of like how Voldemort's minions all vied to be his favorite in the Harry Potter books. It isn't a healthy or happy relationship.

And that is because a bully would rather have people fear them than be rejected. They aren't smart enough to realize the mistake they are making. They are smart enough to understand the power they are creating for themselves, but they don't understand that this isn't helping them create friendships. The way to good friendships is to be a nice person. You don't have to do anything special. You don't have to dress a certain way. You don't have to be like other people. You just have to be nice. Bullies are too afraid to be nice. And that's sad.

## Why This is Important

While it is hard to imagine feeling sorry for someone who is being so mean, there is a good reason to try and feel sorry for a bully. When you feel sorry for bullies, it allows you to respond with compassion instead of fear. This isn't about you. This is about them being so hurt and afraid that they aren't able to act like decent human beings.

When you feel sorry for a bully, you stop being hurt by the things they do and say. And that is reason enough to feel bad for them. Feeling sorry for an abusive person doesn't mean that what they do is OK. It isn't. It is about you no longer being their victim. It is about you replacing your feelings of fear with feelings of sympathy and sorrow for someone else. Which would you rather feel; fear for yourself or sorrow for someone else who is clearly dealing with emotional pain? I know I would rather feel sorry for someone else.

Always remember, you have a choice. Neither is pleasant, and it would be better if you didn't have to deal with this at all, but since you do, you may as well choose to not live in fear. And the way you do that is by choosing to respond with compassion. Consider this a very effective form of mental jujitsu.

## Becoming Fearless

There is a reason why you should accept the fact you are a dork. People who embrace this fact become fearless.

Once you decide that you will not allow petty fearful people (otherwise known as bullies and jerks) to tell you who you are and how you should act and what music you should like and who you should be friends with, you will, without realizing it, start to become fearless.

It all starts with a choice. Yes, the jerks of the world will try to make you feel bad. They will try to tell you there is something wrong with you and they will try to make you behave as they want you to by using fear and threats. They may even physically hurt you in order to control you and instill fear

Whether you are being called names, being threatened, or being stuffed into a locker, the first step is to decide you aren't going to live in fear of your bullies anymore. This is not easy to do. As I said, choosing to not live in fear anymore is just the first step. The rest of this book will provide you with the tools you need to learn how to overcome your fears, to stand up for yourself and what to do if you are physically attacked.

The key to this entire approach is to accept that you are a dork and so what. Once you accept this about yourself, nothing a bully can say to you will change your mind or your behavior since you are no longer afraid of them. In fact, you will feel sorry for them because you recognize them as the sad pathetic individual they are. Once the bullies figure out that you aren't afraid of them, they will pretty much freak out (more on this in the next chapter). The other bonus is that because the last thing a bully wants is your sympathy, they are more likely to stay away from you if that is your response to them. Feeling compassion for a bully really does inoculate you against their behavior.

The coolest part about adopting this strategy is that other people will flock to you once you master it. And that's exactly why the bullies put so much energy into making people afraid. If someone has the courage to calmly stand up to them, they lose power over pretty much everyone else. That someone who has the courage to stand up to them should be you and can be you.

You don't need to worry that you will lose friends. Just the opposite will happen. You will gain friends because of your choice to not be afraid. People like people who don't give in to their fears. They flock to them because it gives them the courage they need to be fearless as well.

And no, you don't have to fight bullies at all. All it takes is one person to stand up and report what happened. If one person has the courage to not be afraid, it helps everyone else respond in the same way. When my son reported that he had been hit on the school bus, his courage to talk about what happened was enough to mobilize all the other kids in his defense. This is a simple matter of there being safety in numbers. One person having the courage to speak out encourages everyone else to speak out as well. This is the only way to break the grip of fear bullies have over your school.

Bullies are only able to operate if there is silent approval of them. The way they get that silent approval is by making people afraid they will be singled out and targeted if they speak out. As soon as one person shows courage in the face of fear, it enables everyone else to stand up against the bullies as well. And again, this isn't about you fighting with a bully. It is about you feeling sorry for the bully so that you no longer respond in fear. One of the best ways to combat fear is through compassion.

How do you get yourself to the point of being fearless? Well, it isn't easy. But ultimately, you have to get yourself to the point that you don't care whether you are a target of a bully or not. And the way you get yourself to that point is to know that you already are a target. It doesn't matter what you do or don't do or how you dress and act. At some point, you are going to be targeted by a bully. All that is needed is for you to be a human.

26

I realize this sounds depressing, but actually, once you accept it, it frees you. Really it does. Accept your worst fear as a reality and you stop being afraid of it. President Franklin Delano Roosevelt once said, "The only thing we have to fear is fear itself." He was right. Once you accept that it doesn't matter what you do you are going to be a target anyway, you free yourself from the worry and the fear of bullies.

At one point in my life I was the victim of a stalker. Stalking is when someone repeatedly bothers you over a period of years. It is a lot like an adult form of bullying. Anyway, I spent three years trying to get the guy to stop bothering me. I got the police involved. I got the FBI involved. I took him to court. Nothing worked. You want to know why? Because he wasn't in control of his behavior. It simply didn't matter what I did or didn't do. He was going to stalk me regardless.

Once I realized this truth and stopped fighting my fear that I couldn't control what was happening to me, it was like a huge weight was lifted. The relief was enormous. I no longer had to try and fix this because it wasn't fixable. Having learned this, I was now free to live my life the way I wanted to because it didn't matter what I did, I was going to be stalked anyway. It turned out that my fear of not being able to get the stalking to stop was **way** worse than the reality of being stalked. Accepting my fate made all the difference for me and freed me from the state of fear I had been living in. Granted, my stalker was not physically violent. But even if he was, being terrified wasn't helping me protect myself from him.

Being a victim of bullying is the same thing. You can't avoid it. That doesn't mean you should just accept the bullying and not do anything about it. It just means that trying to change who you are to avoid being bullied won't work. So, you might as well be the dork you really are. The best revenge you can have is to continue to be your happy dorky self despite how hard they are working to make you afraid of them. An even better revenge is to feel sorry for them because they aren't capable of being truly happy.

# Ignore Them and They Will Go Away

*"Don't pay any attention to the critics - don't even ignore them."*
- Samuel Goldwyn

Let's say you are already being bullied, so it is too late to inoculate yourself. What you need now is a way to get the bullying to stop. The good news is that it is possible to stop the bullying. The bad news is that you have probably already tried to do this and failed.

That's because the way to get a bully to stop is to no longer respond to them. This advice is usually simplified into "ignore them and they will go away." The problem is that "ignore them and they will go away," doesn't ever work.

For obvious reasons, you can't ignore a bully if you go to school with them or ride the bus with them or are in the same class with them. They are where you are and they are in your face and no, you can't just ignore them. They won't let you.

Plus, if you've been told to "ignore them" in the past, you have already tried your best to ignore them and it didn't work. They didn't go away or stop bugging you. In fact, your attempt to ignore them probably made matters worse. So, again, "ignore them and they will go away" is pretty useless advice.

What you really should have been told is that the best way to get bullies to stop bugging you is to not re-enforce them. Do this and they will eventually go away. The problem is that it can take a while. In some cases a very long while. But take heart. This technique really does work; you just need to understand how it works to apply it successfully to your specific bullying problem.

### *Reality vs. Theory*

First things first: whenever you hear "ignore them and they will go away" translate that into "stop rewarding them and they will eventually find someone else to hassle." In order to make this work, you need to know the theory behind this advice, why it will work, what you need to expect, and what exactly you need to do to make it work. Without this information, *stop rewarding them and they will eventually find someone else to hassle* won't work.

So, let's start with the theory behind this advice. I used to train dolphins. I'm a pretty good animal trainer. I've actually trained my cats, which are very hard to train. The good news is that humans are way easier to train than cats. And yes, training does work on humans and *stop rewarding them* is in fact a real training technique. It is called "extinguishing a behavior." It is part of the Operant Conditioning training tool kit.

In order to make *stop rewarding them* work, you do need to understand some of the principles of Operant Conditioning. Here are two online resources you can review for more detailed information:

- Wikipedia Extinction:
  http://en.wikipedia.org/wiki/Extinction_(psychology)
- San Francisco State University – Operant Condition online module:
  http://userwww.sfsu.edu/~psych200/unit3/32.htm

## Operant Conditioning Primer

In the meantime, here is an Operant Conditioning primer. It turns out that all animals, including humans, respond to things that happen to us. Things that happen can be good (positive reinforcement) or bad (negative reinforcement). When we do things that create positive reinforcement, we tend to want to do that thing more and more because it was good for us. If we do something that causes negative reinforcement, we tend to want to do that thing less and less because it was bad for us.

So, for instance, when you are training a dog to sit, you say the word "sit" and then you gently push its bottom down, say good dog and give it a treat. The more you do this, the more the dog will link the act of sitting when you say "sit" to receiving a treat which it considers good. Every time you do this, you are positively reinforcing or rewarding the behavior you want from your dog.

Bullies work in much the same way. You are positively reinforcing or rewarding them every time you emotionally respond to them. The problem is this isn't something you are doing on purpose like you do when you train a dog. Bullies want to get a response out of you. When you respond, that's good for them. It doesn't really matter how you respond. Bullies will treat it as a positive reinforcement. Even when you get mad, which is clearly a negative or bad response; it is still a positive reinforcement from the bully's point of view.

My point is that whether you respond with fear or with anger, you are providing a response to them, and that will be treated as positive reinforcement. Yes, this is rather depressing. It also explains why it is so hard to get bullying to stop.

## How to Extinguish a Behavior

The good news is that it is possible to extinguish a behavior that you don't want. And, you most certainly don't want to be bullied. The problem is that it is very hard to do. But, here's how you do it.

You have to eliminate all reinforcements or rewards for the behavior. This means you need to no longer respond to bullies the way they want you to respond. Ever!

Since bullies tend to treat both positive and negative reinforcement as reinforcement, you need to find a way to do neither. The way to do this in a traditional training setting is to remove yourself from the presence of the animal. As we've discussed, since you live in the real world, keeping yourself away from a bully isn't an option.

The next best thing is to respond to them in a way that is completely devoid of emotion or in an emotion that is not among the responses they were hoping for. If you ever wanted to learn how to be an actor, this is your chance, because in order to pull this off, you need to pretend to not care at all.

It is a good idea to come up with a statement that you can practice and have ready that expresses neither fear, hatred, anger, sadness or any of the other emotions that the bully is hoping to elicit from you.

What you want is something you can say that will not be rude, as that would be a form of reinforcement. You want your statement to express your complete boredom and lack of interest in what the bully is doing or saying. Some examples:
- Really?
- So what?
- I'm sorry, did you say something?
- Or my favorite: Thank you for that information, it is very helpful.

Again, the point is to respond to bullies with as little emotion as possible. The best way to do that is to respond as if they completely bore you. Practice in a mirror to make sure you can pull off a bored expression. If you can throw in a hint of compassion for how pathetic they are, that is a bonus. And yes, feel free to use the exact same expression every single time. It will bore your bullies more quickly.

### For Example:

The first time my son was bullied was in kindergarten. Some of the kids had taken to telling him he was stinky. It really upset him when anyone said that and he didn't like being laughed at. After sniffing him to see if there was any truth to the comments (there wasn't, he smelled just fine), I told him that whenever a kid called him a name, he should look directly at them and say, "thank you for that information, it's really helpful" in as bored a voice as he could manage. I told him that he might have to say it several times, but that whenever someone said something mean, to say this exact phrase every time. We practiced it so that he could say it without a problem.

The next day, sure enough, a couple of the kids in his class started in on him. He delivered his practiced "bored" line and most of the kids just looked at him funny, dropped the subject and went back to their work. Only one kid tried a second time to harass him. My son said the same thing to him, "thank you for that information, it's very helpful." My son said the kid looked confused and gave up. I recently asked him if any of the kids have called him names since then and the answer was no. They hadn't.

The reason they haven't called him names is because he isn't very fun to bully or harass. He doesn't get mad, or sad or angry. He just thanks them for their insult in a bored voice. In other words, he inoculated himself from bullying. This really does work. The bonus is that he became friends with several of the kids who had been harassing him. Kids who bully aren't evil. They are just trying to fit in like everyone else.

## What to Expect

Now that you know how to behave in a way that actually allows you to no longer reward a bully when they bug you, now what? Well, now comes the hard part. It turns out that when you are extinguishing a behavior what you are really doing is no longer providing the positive reinforcement that your bully has been receiving for his or her efforts. What comes next is known as a blowout or extinction burst.

What this means in plain English is that the bullying is going to get worse before it gets better. Here's why. When an animal is used to something working, they don't like it very much when it stops working. The more suddenly it stops working, the more frantic they are to get it working again and the harder they try to get it to work.

For instance, if you trained a rat to press a lever and every time it pressed that lever, you gave it food. Then suddenly the lever stopped working for the rat, it wouldn't just think – hey, the lever doesn't work anymore, I think I'll go do something else. No, the standard response for all animals, including humans, is to press the lever more and more until the animal is pressing that lever almost constantly. Don't believe me? Consider what every single human does when a vending machine doesn't work.

Eventually, if the food lever/vending machine continues to not work, the rat will give up. But the point is the rat is not going to give up without a fight. Bullies won't either.

If you were to graph the rat's response to its lever not working, it would look something like this:

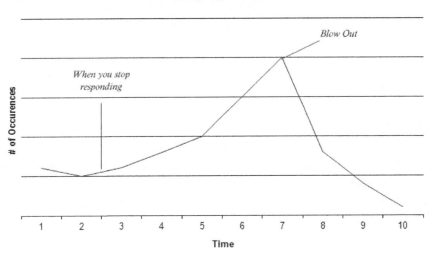

**Extinquishing Behavior**

The rat will realize the lever isn't working and will get really aggressive with the lever to try and make it work, causing a spike in its behavior. Eventually, it will give up and stop trying.

This graph shows the same pattern of behavior that will occur when you stop responding to bullies. Their obnoxious behavior is rather steady until you stop responding to them. Once you stop responding to bullies the way they want, their obnoxious behavior spikes and becomes more frequent and more severe as they try to get you to respond. This is known as a blowout. If the blowout fails to get the desired response, their attempts will fall off quite rapidly. Eventually they stop trying altogether.

The good news is that the blowout means you are close to extinguishing the behavior. The bad news is that because we are all humans with real human emotions, rather than a broken vending machine, most people give in at this point and respond to the bullying.

Keep in mind, this only really works for verbal abuse or threatened violence. If you are being hit, punched, kicked, slammed into a locker, or having your stuff stolen and thrown in the trash, you will need to treat the problem as a criminal matter, which is covered in the next chapter.

### Staying Strong

The problem you will run into is that at some point the bully will be needling you so much to get you to respond, you may have a moment of weakness and respond in an emotional way to them.

In order to make this work, you need to understand the concept of reinforcement schedules. It turns out that how often you give an animal reinforcement impacts how strongly they associate your response with their behavior. Contrary to common sense, it turns out that a variable reinforcement schedule creates a much stronger association than a regular reinforcement schedule.

Let me translate that into plain English for you. Rewarding an animal all the time is less effective than giving out the rewards at random. The more random the rewards are, the stronger the behavior becomes. Yes, this seems strange, but this is really how it works.

For instance, when you are first starting to train a dog to sit, you will give them food every time they sit on command. This helps establish the behavior you want. However, once the dog is trained to sit, it is actually better to give them food every once in a while, instead of every time. Because, if the dog is assured it will get a treat every time it sits, then when it isn't interested in the treat, it isn't going to be all that interested in sitting for you. An animal is more willing to sit if it isn't sure if it will get a treat or not. Most animals would rather sit in the hopes that this might be one of the times they get a treat than take the chance on a future treat that may or may not come.

## What this Means for You and Your Bullies.

Because bullies are human, they respond to variable or random reinforcements the same way a dog does. This means that if sometimes you respond to them and sometimes you don't, they will want to bully you more, not less.

If you "ignore" bullies by not responding to them in the way they want, and then start responding to them again you make your situation worse. In training terms, all you will have taught them is that in order to get you to respond, they need to be really super obnoxious. So they will be. For them, putting in the extra effort required to get you to respond is better than having their little rat lever/vending machine stop working entirely.

What you actually want them to learn is that it doesn't matter how obnoxious they are, you aren't going to give them the response they want. Ever! This requires you to not respond to them the way they want regardless of how obnoxious they become. And that's really hard to do because they can become really obnoxious.

I realize that continuing to maintain your calm in the face of bullying that has become super obnoxious is extremely hard to do. However, you either keep calm and refuse to respond, or you give in and not only continue the cycle of bullying, you make the bullying worse.

### *How Long Will it Take?*

It can take a long time: longer than you want and longer than you should have to endure it. For instance, when I started ignoring my stalker it took about two years for him to stop, though he periodically would attempt to get my attention for several years afterwards.

Generally speaking, the longer bullies bully, the longer it will take them to stop. This is why it is important to stop the bullying before it starts. It is easier to prevent bullying than it is to extinguish it.

36

Even after the bullying behavior is extinguished, a bully will occasionally push your buttons on the off chance that you will respond just as people will occasionally try a vending machine they know to be broken. Should you have to deal with this? No. But if you are being bullied, you have no choice. So stop feeling sorry for yourself and do what you need to do to get it to stop. Be consistent. Don't re-enforce them, and continue to report them to your teachers.

Don't let the fact that it can take a couple of years scare you. The benefits to this approach aren't just in getting your harasser(s) to stop. Your stress levels will drop way sooner than that. I have no idea when my stalker actually stopped because I was no longer paying attention to him.

At the beginning, I just pretended not to pay attention to him. But a funny thing happened as I gained more practice in not paying attention to him. I actually stopped paying attention to him for real. I simply stopped caring what he did or didn't do. Even though he continued his obnoxious behavior for a couple of years, it didn't impact me in the same way it had when I was paying attention to him out of fear. In fact, I don't even remember him blowing out. I'm sure he did, but I wasn't paying enough attention to him to notice it. This approach doesn't just stop the person harassing you; it saves your sanity in the process.

The problem is how long it takes to get to the blowout and how long and severe blowouts really are. It is very hard to respond in an unemotional way when a bully reaches the blowout phase because blowouts can be really hard. However, that is when it is most important that you don't respond emotionally to them. The good news is that once you stop responding to bullies and they get to the point they are blowing out, you are nearly done.

From a training standpoint, the longer an animal has been getting their expected reward, and the more random the rewards are, the longer it will take to extinguish the behavior and the more aggressive the animal will be to get their reward back.

In other words, the longer bullies haves been bullying the longer it is going to take to get them to stop. This is why if it is at all possible, the sooner you can start being emotionally neutral in your response to bullies, the better.

If you have been bothered by bullies for a long while and you have tried to ignore them, but found that the bullying just got worse, so you gave in, and now you have read this and realized, oh crap, I made things worse. Don't be too hard on yourself.

What you do going forward is what matters now. Adopt a "non-responsive" strategy, cultivate an "I don't care attitude" towards the things your bully is doing and commit yourself to riding out the blowout to come. You will be glad you did! Because this really does work and it is worth it. Because on the other side of this journey is freedom and the knowledge that you can tackle anything life throws at you.

## Support and Social Media

When you adopt an, a *stop rewarding them* approach to a bully, you need to make that complete. That means that your bullies should not get any information that they have succeeded in getting to you from you anywhere. Don't post how they are making you feel on Facebook. Don't post videos on YouTube about how upset they are making you. As far as social media is concerned, if your bullies have access to it, don't post it, text it or IM it. You need to give your bullies the impression that they aren't worth your time or attention. This requires you to not talk about them in social settings where word could get back to your bullies that yes, indeed, they are bothering you.

You also need to be careful about who you confide in. Anyone who might report back to the bully about your emotional state, or who might tell a friend who tells a friend who tells the bully about how you are really feeling is someone you can't confide in. We're talking total information blackout. As far as the bully is concerned, you need to *show* them they aren't getting to you. Yes, this takes some effort. Yes, you do have to hide the emotional impact they are having on you from certain people. And yes that means not being totally honest about how you feel.

This does not mean that you should not confide in people or share your emotions about how hurt you are with others. You must do that for your sanity. You just need to find outlets you can trust to keep your situation confidential. It means you have to pick the people you trust very carefully. Because if your bullies get wind that they have gotten to you, however remotely they come by that information, they will count that as positive reinforcement that their evil deeds are working.

So, who can you trust? Your parents, your aunts, uncles, the school counselor, cousins, secure networks with people who don't know any of the kids in your school. There are places and ways to get the support you need without letting your bullies know how they are making you feel. You need to find them and use them.


## If You Really Must

If you really must comment on their behavior on social media, make sure that you do so only in passing and with the same bored, barely worth your time, but you do feel sorry for them attitude you have been cultivating in relationship to them. Again, you don't need to be mean or catty about what is going on. You just need to keep all comments about them in a "you feel sorry for them" framework.

I am a public figure and a writer. I get nasty people who post nasty things on my websites and essays all the time. They are called trolls. Some people just think it is fun to say mean things about other people. However, they don't pester me much because I don't respond to them. I don't delete their posts. I don't write anything in response. In short, I don't do anything. I act as if they never posted. Why? Because trolls aren't worth my time.

Because I don't give them my time, they don't waste time on me. Their insults don't bother me at all. I understand it isn't about me. I was actually chosen at random. They are just trying to get a response. Don't give them a response and they really do go away. Eventually. In the meantime, everyone else is able to see what trolls they are by virtue of how rude and mean they are being. By not responding you remain calm, cool, and collected. You will be seen as a compassionate person of courage that other people will envy. Even if it is just an act to start out with, you will eventually start to own the person you are becoming, who is fearless in the face of jerks.

### Don't Feed the Beast

Hopefully by now you will have a firm grasp of exactly how a *stop rewarding them* strategy works, why it works, how to implement it and what to expect from your bullies in response to this strategy. There are, however, a couple of other tidbits of advice you should know about.

The first is that the sooner you stop rewarding bullies, the quicker they will stop. The longer the bullying has been going on the more entrenched the behavior of your bully is and the harder they are going to fight to make bullying work for them again. If you are in a chronic situation that has been going on for a period of years, you may want to consider spending a few weeks weakening your bully's attachment to bullying you before you start your "non-reinforcement" strategy.

## Consistency is Key

If you have been bullied for a long period of time, you are probably variably reinforcing your bully. Sometimes you respond. Sometimes you don't. This variable reinforcement makes a bully want to bully more and thus it makes it harder to extinguish the bullying.

When trainers set out to extinguish an entrenched behavior, the first thing they usually do is make the reinforcement for the behavior they want to extinguish regular or consistent. This is counter intuitive because your real goal is to no longer reward them at all. However, what taking this extra step does is it weakens the animal's attachment to the behavior, making it easier to extinguish when you do eventually start your non-reinforcement strategy.

What this means in plain English is that if you spend a couple of weeks consistently reinforcing your bully prior to starting your *non-responsive* strategy, it will pay off in a shorter and slightly less severe blow out period. Again, this is for chronic situations only where a couple of weeks aren't going to make much of a difference. For newer and less established problems, all you need to do is stop reinforcing/rewarding them.

In order to make this work, you need to come up with a standard emotional response to the bullying. It could be an angry look, it could be a snarky comment or you could run away dramatically in tears yelling, "I'm going to tell a teacher on you." Don't be mean, just be consistent and give them the exact same response every time you are hassled by them and do this for a couple of weeks. They will be confused, but they will be unlikely to escalate since they are still getting a response from you. It just won't be nearly as fun for them because it will be so predictable and regular.

After a couple of weeks, change to your chosen *stop reinforcing/rewarding them* tactic. Again, you need to be consistent doing the exact same thing every single time. No wavering. The more consistent you are, the sooner they will cycle through to a blowout and ultimately give up on you.

This is an optional tactic that you should only consider if your situation is chronic and long term. Again, the reason you may want to try this is to weaken your bully's desire to bully you. By consistently responding for a couple of weeks you weaken a bully's compulsion by putting them on a regular reinforcement schedule. Once you switch to your chosen *stop reinforcing/rewarding them* strategy, they will be less attached to bullying you and will give it up more easily.

## The Flip Side

In addition to no longer responding to the bad behavior of a bully, you will also want to consider adding a positive reinforcement response if by some miracle they exhibit good behavior. If they are nice to you, thank them and be nice back. Have something nice planned to say to them. If they are rude, respond with your standard *I will no longer reinforce your bad behavior* tactic.

There is a very good reason for doing this. When animal trainers are working on extinguishing a behavior in an animal, they almost always provide the animal with an alternate behavior they want to see happen. For instance, if we no longer want our rat to get food by pressing a lever, we stop providing food when it presses a lever. If we want to make it easier for

41

the rat to give up its lever and to reduce the inevitable blowout, we have to provide it with an alternate way to get food.

When we apply this tactic to bullies, we see that what bullies want is our attention. The only time you should give them your attention is when they are being nice. This means you need to catch them being nice. I know that's hard to do because when they aren't bugging you, you would probably prefer to be as far away from them as possible. It is just that the sooner they learn they will get more out of you from being nice than being mean, the sooner they will give up on being mean. So, don't take those moments when your bullies aren't being mean for granted. Make sure to say something nice to them in those moments. It could be as simple as a smile, or saying hi, or thanking them for something.

When you first start providing positive reinforcement for good behavior, bullies will most likely revert back to being mean to you on the spot. That's normal. They don't know how to relate to you in a civil way so they fall back on their bullying behavior. It is easier for them and it is what they know and again, it always worked for them in the past. When they do this, give them your standard non-reinforcement response and move on as if nothing unusual happened.

Remember what I said at the beginning of this book. Most bullies bully because they are afraid that if they don't bully you, you will bully them so they are mean to pretty much everyone as a way to defend themselves. It is a very sad way to go through life. By being nice to them in those few precious moments when they are being good, you are helping them learn that, no, you aren't going to be mean to them and they don't have anything to fear from you. It really can turn things around for them.

The beauty of doing this is that it puts you in control. Yes, they are still being mean, but you are the one in control of the situation, not them. In short, you are training your bullies to not be such jerks. That's pretty darned cool when you think about it. The bonus is that you get to be the cool, calm, collected individual who was able to find compassion for the rudest jerks in the school. And that's something to be proud of.

Keep doing this and eventually, if your bullies are smart, they will transition into being relatively nice to you sooner rather than later. Because the sooner you give an animal an alternative way to get reinforced and the more positive that reinforcement is, the sooner it gives up the behavior you don't like and the less extreme the blowout will be. Bullies will still have a blowout and they will still try to get you to go back to the old pattern of behaving where they bully you and you cower. It is just that the blowout won't be quite as bad.

## To Recap

- Do not reward others for bullying behavior

- The sooner you stop rewarding bullies, the quicker they will stop.

- Report all bullying to a trusted adult

- The longer the bullying has been going on, the more entrenched the behavior of your bullies is and the harder they are going to fight to make bullying work for them again.

- If you are in a chronic situation that has been going on for a period of years, you may want to consider spending a few weeks weakening your bully's attachment to bullying you before you start your "non-reinforcement" strategy.

- Positively reinforce good behavior whenever a bully does something nice.

- Be consistent in applying this method.

- Do not discuss the bully on social media or with people you can't trust.

This method will not only help you deal with bullying, you will discover, with time, that you will be braver, stronger, more confident, and have the type of character that draws people to you.

# Getting Help

*"Remember, if you ever need a helping hand, it is at the end of your arm. As you get older, remember you have another hand: the first is to help yourself, the second is to help others."*

- Audrey Hepburn

Up to this point, the sort of bullying I have been talking about is mostly verbal or emotional. It involves teasing, taunts, verbal threats and other obnoxious but basically non-violent acts.

The problem is that bullying can sometimes involve fists, sticks and stones. You can be physically hurt by bullying. If you have been hurt or are in danger of physical assault, you need to know what your rights are, what can be done to intervene on your behalf and who can help you.

### Report, Report, Report and then Report Some More!

Regardless of what sort of bullying you are experiencing or witnessing, to get help, you need to ask for it. This means you need to tell an adult what is happening. Reporting a bully is not snitching or tattling. It is the right thing to do because a bully is causing harm and unless they are stopped, the violence and fear is going to continue.

Bullies will try to intimidate you into not snitching on them because they don't want to get in trouble for what they are doing. But in order to get the bullying to stop, you need to get them in trouble. This is what it means to stand up to a bully. It means reporting them.

Don't assume because you have told a teacher that there is a problem that this will solve it. It won't. As we discussed before in the previous chapter, bullies will continue to try and bully because their efforts at bullying have been rewarding for them in terms of power and status gained from their efforts. In order to get rid of those rewards, you need to report each and every instance of bullying and harassment you see or experience. Your reporting efforts compliment your non-reinforcing strategy. You need to report and not reinforce your bullies at the same time. You do not report on bullying to harm the bullies or to get back at them. You report them out of genuine concern that they are not only harming someone, but that they are harming themselves by being obnoxious.

Bullies need to learn that their actions have consequences and that when they treat other people with respect they will be rewarded and that when they harm, hurt or intimidate other people they will be punished. The only way for them to learn how to behave in a respectful way is to make sure that every time they are mean, they get punished. Reporting them really is a compassionate thing to do.

And again, expect things to get worse before they get better. Also, expect them to direct their anger at you for "getting them in trouble." Just keep reporting them and using your favorite non-reinforcement strategy with them. Stay the course and eventually they will blowout and give up.

## Extreme Circumstances

It is possible that you may need more help than your school can provide. This is often the case if you have been bullied for a long period of time or if the school has failed to help you. Additionally, if you are being hit or physically hurt, you may want to consider other ways you can get help.

## The Law is on Your Side

The most interesting aspect about bullying is that if this behavior happened in the adult world, it would be treated as a criminal act and law enforcement would be brought in to deal with it. For some reason, what kids do in school is often viewed by many adults as just kids being kids. You might be left on your own to deal with stuff adults wouldn't dream of dealing with on their own.

However, just because you are a kid doesn't mean you aren't protected by the same laws that protect adults. You just need to know what those laws are and how to get law enforcement and the legal system to come to your aid if you need it.

A word of caution: do not assume that law enforcement is going to solve your problem. It won't. It is just another tool you can use to help you deal with a situation that no one should have to deal with.

Calling the cops is probably the quickest way to make your bullies really mad at you. It will justify their angry feelings towards you and help them rationalize their bad behavior. If you do decide to call the cops, you need to understand that doing so will make things worse for a while. However, just as with any blowout, it may be worth it to ride out the storm that comes from taking this action. Only you can decide whether it is worth it or not.

### Specific Laws:

There are some specific laws that cover the behavior of bullies. The crimes in question are stalking, assault, and battery. You will also want to know about the option of getting a restraining order.

Because of how difficult it is to pursue legal charges against someone, you should probably only consider seeking legal assistance when your other options have failed to control the problem or if what has happened was so dangerous and extreme that criminal charges really are warranted.

In other words, I am providing this information, not as legal advice, but as a way to help you a) learn what your legal rights are and b) learn how to talk more effectively about what it is you are experiencing so that the adults you are asking for help, understand what it is you are experiencing.

## Stalking

I live in Florida and according to Florida criminal law, "any person who willfully, maliciously, and repeatedly follows or harasses another person commits the offense of stalking," which is considered a first degree misdemeanor. That means if someone is convicted of stalking they could be fined up to $1,000 and/or get up to one year in jail.

If the person stalking you also threatens you with bodily injury, it is considered aggravated stalking which is a third degree felony punishable by a $5,000 fine and/or up to five years in jail.

In other words, when an adult is harassed for a long period of time it, isn't called bullying, it is called stalking. All that is required is for this to not be a one-time thing where someone calls you a name. If it is an ongoing pattern of harassment it isn't bullying. It is stalking, it's illegal and the person doing it can go to jail.

The problem obviously is that most cops won't treat school yard bullying as stalking. And many adults are in the habit of dismissing the problems that kids who are being bullied are facing.

If what is happening to you is extreme and constant, then you might want to consider relabeling what is happening to you as stalking instead of bullying. Make the point that this isn't just bullying you are experiencing, what is happening to you is a criminal level of harassment that should be treated as a criminal offense worthy of law enforcement involvement.

Every state has a stalking law so, wherever you live, you have some legal protection against what is in fact a crime. Check out the Stalking Resource Center to find out what the law is where you live: http://www.ncvc.org/src/main.aspx?dbID=DB_State-byState_Statutes117. Knowing what your rights are is the first step in being able to demand them.

## Assault

In Florida where I live, an "assault" is defined as "an intentional, unlawful threat by word or act to do violence to the person of another, coupled with an apparent ability to do so, and doing some act which creates a well-founded fear in such other person that such violence is imminent." In other words, if someone threatens you and you think you are in physical danger that is considered assault. It is a second degree misdemeanor punishable by a fine of up to $500 and/or up to sixty days in jail.

Aggravated assault is an assault that involves some sort of deadly weapon. If someone threatens you with a gun in their hands or a stick that could kill you, even if it were an accident, that is aggravated assault. It is considered a third degree felony which is punishable with a fine up to $5,000 and/or five years in jail.

Again, this information is being provided so that you are able to properly name what is happening to you. When you say, "I was bullied," to the average adult, it doesn't give us the same level of understanding about what has happened to you as when you say "I was assaulted."

Keep in mind that most adults think of assault as a physical attack. It isn't. It is actually just the threat of an attack and yes, just threatening someone with violence is a crime. Again, knowing your rights is the first step in demanding they be respected.

## Battery

A physical attack is a crime called "battery;" and in Florida battery is a felony defined as actually and intentionally touching or striking another person against the will of the other; or intentionally causing bodily harm to another person. This is considered a first degree felony punishable by a fine of up to $10,000 and/or up to ten years in jail. In other words, anyone who hits you or hurts you is guilty of a very serious crime.

If they use a weapon or cause great bodily harm, permanent disability or disfigurement, it is considered aggravated battery. This is a second degree felony which is punishable by up to $10,000 in fines and/or up to fifteen years in prison.

If you are strangled during the attack, where someone tries to prevent you from breathing that could be considered a third degree felony, which is punishable with a fine up to $5,000 and up to five years in jail.

If someone hits you and you didn't give them permission to hit you, it is a crime and they can and should be punished for it. When you tell an adult what happened, don't just say I was bullied or harassed. If you have been hit, punched, kicked or otherwise hurt, you are a victim of a battery and what happened to you is a crime.

When you talk to an adult about this, make sure they understand you were assaulted. Even though the technical term is battered, most adults will understand assault to mean a physical attack and you are more likely to get them to help you than if you just say you were bullied or harassed.

### Legal Remedies

Don't think because you are a kid you cannot press criminal charges against someone else. You can with your parent's help. Whether you want to do this or not is something you will need to discuss with your parents. It is at least something to discuss as a possibility.

If you aren't sure whether or not this is the right course of action for you, consider this: if you are being harassed and/or assaulted and/or physically attacked, you probably aren't the only one in your school suffering.

When my son was in kindergarten, he was attacked by a third grader on the bus who hit him in the head so hard his vision went blurry. It turned out my son was the sixth kid on that bus who had been hit by that same kid. The school encouraged me to press battery charges against the child who hit my son. It opened my eyes up to the fact that, yes, criminal charges can and sometimes should be brought against school bullies.

Understand that getting involved with the legal system is a hassle and can be very upsetting to everyone involved. Seeking justice isn't easy. It takes commitment. The process will be very hard. It will cost a lot. It is not a decision you should take without just cause. Also, it can make the bully who assaulted you that much madder at you and that much more likely to assault you further.

However, in some cases, it is the best thing you can do, not only for yourself, but for the bully as well. The kid who hit my son had an absent mother and was doing everything he could do to get in trouble. Again, it wasn't just my son who was attacked by this child, others were as well. When it comes to behavior that isn't just verbal harassment, but crosses over into assault and battery, your school has limited resources it can use to deal with what might actually be a criminal matter. If what is happening has risen to the level of a crime, you are doing everyone a favor by pressing charges to make it a criminal matter as opposed to just a school discipline issue.

## Document

In order to press charges you will need to provide proof that what is happening has risen to the level of stalking, assault and/or battery. Without proof the legal system can't help you. In order to convict someone of a crime, the prosecutor needs to be able to prove that the crime occurred and that the person charged with committing the crime did it. This needs to be proven beyond a reasonable doubt.

Don't expect anyone else to do this for you. Yes, the police should investigate and provide the proof that is needed. The problem is that without physical evidence such as videotape, bruising or other evidence of the attack, all they have is your word against the person who hurt you. That isn't enough. You need to be able to prove what happened and not just ask people to take you at your word.

This really is important. In my son's case, we weren't able to press charges because the camera on the bus that should have recorded the battery against my son wasn't working so we had no proof it happened. Even though the kid admitted to hitting my son it wasn't enough to convict him in a court of law. We needed the evidence that the video tape log from the bus would have provided.

Find out if the school has cameras. If they do, every single time something happens, request that the footage be provided. Do the same with the school buses. If someone is sending you harassing emails or posting threats about you on the web, make copies of them for proof. Keep a log of everything that happens, from the mundane snarky comments to the outright physical attacks. If you are being bullied, the most likely law that will apply is the stalking law. Stalking requires you to prove a pattern of harassment, which means a single incident isn't enough to get law enforcement involved. The more you can document or make a list of every time you are harassed, assaulted or hit, the more law enforcement will take you seriously.

Good documentation consists of a list of dates and times when something occurred, where it occurred, a description of what happened, a list of witnesses who saw it happen along with whatever other supporting evidence may be available from video tapes to photos. Keep a list of everything that happens and it will help you get the bullying under control because it will help adults better understand the severity of what is happening to you.

## Restraining Orders

This brings us to the topic of restraining orders. Most states provide you with the option to get what is called a "protective injunction against repeat violence," also known as a restraining order. Check your state law to see what the requirements are. In Florida you can get an "injunction against repeat violence" if someone has committed two acts of violence against you during the six months prior to you requesting the injunction.

In Florida, "Violence means any assault, aggravated assault, battery, aggravated battery, sexual assault, sexual battery, stalking, aggravated stalking, kidnapping, or false imprisonment, or any criminal offense resulting in physical injury or death, by a person against any other person."

If you are being bullied, you should easily qualify for a restraining order. All you have to do is provide evidence of at least two times you have experienced harassment level stalking, threats of violence or actual incidences of violence against you in a six-month period.

In order for you to get one, your parent or legal guardian will need to file the paperwork on your behalf and in order to do that they must have witnessed the violence against you themselves, have physical evidence of the violence and/or have sworn affidavits from eyewitnesses that the violence against you is occurring. Again, it means, if you are going to go this route, you will need to document what is happening and get assistance from the adults around you so that you can prove that it is happening, and that can be a bit tricky.

It can also cost you and your parents some money. For instance, in my son's case, in order to prove that he was hit hard enough to cause a concussion, we would have needed to go to a doctor to have him examined so that we could prove that he had gotten a concussion. Saying he was hit that hard isn't enough. It has to be proven. If physical injury has occurred, getting a doctor to document the injuries is extremely helpful!

This will also cost money because while your parent or legal guardian can file this paperwork on your behalf, your petition still needs to be heard by a judge and you would benefit from having a trained lawyer make your case for you in court. Yes, your parent can represent you in court. Technically you don't need to hire a lawyer to plead your case to a judge. However, I made that mistake one time when dealing with my stalker and will never make it again. You really do need a lawyer to represent you.

Additionally, a lawyer can advise you and your parents on the specific laws of your state and what sort of documentation you may need in order to get a judge to grant your request for protection.

## The benefits of a restraining order/injunction

Getting a restraining order has several benefits. First, the fact you are seeking one will let bullies know that you aren't going to allow them to bully you anymore. Yes, it will make the bullies angry, but they may be less likely to physically hurt you once they know there is a legal record of your complaint against them. Depending on how smart or stupid the bullies are, it may take them being hauled into court for violating a restraining order for them to understand what exactly the consequences of hassling you are.

Another benefit to getting a restraining order is that once it is granted, the person you have requested protection from is legally prohibited from interacting with you. The bullies can't call you, harass you, contact you (directly or indirectly), or continue to commit violence against you without committing a crime because, in Florida, it is a first degree felony to violate a restraining order. In other words, having a restraining order is a form of documentation that provides a legal basis for further protection.

A third benefit is that it is easier to get a restraining order than it is to press criminal charges because the standard of proof is lower. You just need to show reasonable cause, which means there only needs to be enough evidence that any reasonable person would agree that you are being harassed, stalked, assaulted or attacked.

Finally, by getting a restraining order you provide a legal framework which will allow your school and law enforcement to take the steps needed to protect you from harm. That means that the school will be provided with the legal means to remove your bully from your classroom, prevent them from being on the playground at the same time as you, and more. Without that restraining order, a school is limited in what can be done because school officials have no legal right to restrict the actions of a student without just cause. With the restraining order they not only can protect you, they must.

## A word of caution

If you get a restraining order, don't expect it to protect you. If your bully is intent on harming you, a piece of paper isn't going to stop them. All that an injunction does is give the police the ability to deal with the violence committed against you after the fact. In other words, after you get a restraining order, if your bully continues to commit violence against you, you now have a legal framework to pursue help. However, documenting the abuse/violence will still probably be up to you.

## *What to Do When No One Takes You Seriously?*

The biggest hurdle you will face in getting adults to help you with your bullying situation is to get the adults around you to understand that what is happening is really bad and that it really is something they should be helping you with.

It is often hard for adults to grasp this. There are several reasons why. I am going to provide some examples so you can better understand why adults may at first ignore what you are telling them. The point of this is for you to understand what you need to do to explain your situation to adults so that they will pay attention.

The first reason an adult might ignore you is because conflicts among people of any age are normal. Everyone needs to learn how to deal with these conflicts on their own. If you don't learn how to deal with everyday conflicts between people on your own, you will be at a disadvantage later in life. However, if you are being bullied, what is happening isn't just ordinary conflict. It is a pattern of harassment that may be criminal. To get past this, you need to keep a record of every interaction that happens so that the adults around you can be shown that this isn't a normal conflict. This is something you can't deal with on your own.

Another reason why adults might not get involved is because you have no evidence to back up your claims. If you tell adults someone hit you, they will take that seriously, but they also have to consider whether or not you are lying to get someone else in trouble. Don't take this personally. The fact of the matter is that some people lie. If adults can't find any evidence that what you said occurred, they are going to err on the side of caution and not take any action at all. No one wants to punish someone for something they didn't do. If this seems unfair to you, consider how you would feel if someone accused you of hitting someone when you didn't. You would want the adults in authority to give you the benefit of the doubt, wouldn't you? In order to get past this hurdle, you need to provide evidence that what you say happened, really happened. You either need to get other students to corroborate, or you need to show other evidence.

Finally, some adults just can't be bothered. Dealing with bullying is not something any adult wants to deal with and some adults will indeed stick their heads in the sand and ignore what is happening, even when you present them with evidence. There are many reasons why an adult might ignore the abuse that you are enduring. If the first adult you talk to ignores you, you need to find another adult who will.

## At Your School

If your teacher ignores your concerns, go to the school counselor or nurse and tell them what is happening. If they ignore you, try the principal or vice principal. Keep a log of each time you talk to an adult at the school and what they said to you about your concerns. You may need that later.

If the teachers at the school don't help, ask your parents or another trusted adult to advocate on your behalf.

## Your Parents

You will also want to let your parents know. Again, keeping a log of everything that is happening will help your parents help you. Without your log of what you are enduring, they don't have anything they can use to put pressure on the school to better protect you. Without that log, they do not have the evidence they need to help you navigate the legal system on your behalf. If your parents refuse to help you, find another relative that will, whether it is an aunt, uncle, grandparent or other legal guardian.

## Youth Groups

Most counties have a variety of youth groups, whether it is the Police Athletic League or a community program. If, for some reason, you have failed to get the school administrators to help you and your parents can't be bothered, try reaching out to a youth counselor at one of the youth programs in your area. They may just be the advocate you need. Again, your log/list of what has been happening will be invaluable to you.

## Police

It shouldn't come to this, but if your attempts to get help from the school and your parents fail, which can happen on very rare occasions, or even when everyone is working hard to protect you, you may want to reach out to the police or sheriff's office. Once again, you are going to need your log of what is happening to you for them to even begin to offer help. Without that log and your documentation, there is nothing the police can do for you.

The other law enforcement person who may be able to help is the prosecutor's office. Most counties have a victim's assistance program to help you navigate the legal system if it comes to that. If all these attempts fail, consider writing a letter to the juvenile court judge in your county explaining your situation and provide them with a copy of your bullying log.

# Exceptional Cases

*"Bigotry and judgment are the height of insecurity."*

        -    Jasmine Guy

There are two types of bullying that need to be dealt with separately. These are religious bullying and sexual bullying. Most of the recent suicides caused by bullying seem to have resulted from a toxic mixture of religious and sexual bullying. Being singled out for your religious beliefs and/or your sexual identity can be extremely hard to deal with since both are so central to who you are as a person.

### Religious Bullying

If you are a person of faith and someone tells you that you are an affront to God and that God is going to send you to burn in hell, that's a very upsetting thing to hear.

The sad fact of life is that for some people, religion isn't about learning to love and respect others; it is about learning to hate and demonize others. If anyone ever tells you that they know what God's will is and that God hates you, they have just proven that they believe God wants them to hate. That is very sad and very wrong.

## What you need to know

These are not people you can reason with. You can't argue with them that they are wrong so don't even try. Please don't think for a minute that they might be right. They aren't. They don't know what they are talking about. They are just parroting what they learned in their church, which is apparently a hate-filled church. Most importantly, what they are trying to do is gain social status by being "holier than thou," which is a sure sign that they aren't.

The best way to deal with such people is to feel sorry for them because they don't understand what it means to love their neighbors. This approach will help you feel better immediately and it will help you ignore their taunts more easily.

If you must respond to these holier than thou types, the best way is to compassionately call them out on their self-righteousness and walk away. It doesn't matter if they claim to speak with religious authority; the fact is they are *not*. They are kids just like you. All they have learned to do is quote some out-of-context Bible verses that they don't even understand fully. But if they can convince you to be afraid of their "religious authority" they can get status among their religious friends and the leaders of their church.

As hard as it is to ignore religious taunts and threats, you must. People who throw their hate-filled beliefs in other people's faces are guilty of religious hubris, which means that they are guilty of excessive pride and arrogance. Do you really think such jerks are speaking for God? I don't.

No one knows what God's will is or if He or She even has a will. NO ONE! Anyone who claims to know is either lying or deluded. If people are trying to gain social status because of their perceived piousness, they are guilty of the sin of pride because they have made it clear by their actions that they care more for their social status than they do about God's teachings. The Bible is very clear on this. God doesn't like pride. He loves the humble.

The best way to deal with this sort of religious taunting is again, to call them out politely and compassionately and simply walk away. Here are a couple of quotes you may use. And no – you don't need to explain them to religious bullies. Heck, you don't even have to give them the actual quote. You can just provide the verse numbers and encourage them to look it up for themselves. *Don't ever get sucked into an argument with holier than thou people.* Show your humble wisdom by holding your tongue. If you give them a Bible quote they don't know you will force them to admit they don't know or understand the Bible as well as they think they do and that is often all it takes to make them more humble in the future or at least to go find other targets to hassle.

## From Proverbs

Proverbs 11:2 – When pride cometh, then cometh shame: but with the lowly is wisdom.
Proverbs: 11:12 – He that is void of wisdom despiseth his neighbor: but a man of understanding holdeth his peace.

## From Luke 18

If your bully argues the above quotes are from the Old Testament and that they only abide by the teachings of Jesus in the New Testament; say, Jesus felt the same way and refer them to Luke 18:9 – 14 which is a parable about the sin of pride as told by Jesus.

Luke 18:9 - And he spake this parable unto certain which trusted in themselves that they were righteous and despised others.
Luke 18:14 - For every one that exalteth himself shall be abased; and he that humbleth himself shall be exalted.

There are many more quotes in the Bible about pride and online Bible searches can help you find them. But again, you will be more effective if you just use one or two as a standard response to those who think they know more about the Bible and God's will than anyone else. Sounding like a broken record is exactly what will make them want to leave you alone. Just keep referring these arrogant fools to the same tired quotes and ignore any of their attempts to claim that they are right on this matter or that their obnoxious behavior is justified. They aren't right and there is never a good reason to be a jerk. End of story.

## Religious Minorities

Americans are very diverse and as a general rule we respect the right of people to believe differently than us. According to the Americans Religious Identification Survey (http://commons.trincoll.edu/aris/) about 76% of Americans are Christian, about 12% are atheist and the remaining 12% may be a member of a variety of other faith including Buddhist, Jewish, Islamic, Hindu, Pagan and a host of other belief systems. Among those who self-label as Christians, there are literally a few hundred different denominations of Christianity practiced in America and no, they don't all believe the same things.

Long story short: Americans are a religiously diverse people. I bring this up because there is a good likelihood that at some point, you will be bullied for not believing the same things that your peers do. Most of the time, this sort of bullying is focused on religious minorities, otherwise known as the 24% of the country that isn't Christian. If you find yourself being singled out for not being Christian, you are not alone.

The good news is that according to a study done by researchers at the University of California at Berkeley[3] 75% of Americans feel that whatever it is you believe is OK. This means that most people are quite happy to get along with people of differing beliefs.

The bad news is that leaves 25% (or one in four) who are not OK with you not believing as they do. That 25% can be really vocal and really obnoxious. The other bad news is that if you try to claim your right to not believe as the majority, that 25% will become very angry. It isn't unusual for some of them to start issuing death threats. These won't just come from your fellow students; their parents will issue their own death threats as well. This is well documented and very predictable behavior. I personally have several friends who have been threatened this way. One in particular has to travel under a fake name for her protection.

The trick to ignoring the 25% who haven't figured out that America is the land of the free and that our first and most important freedom is religious freedom is to realize that a) these people are idiots and: b) they are not worth your time worrying about. The reason I say this is because they are equal opportunity oppressors. When they aren't hassling non-Christians for not being Christian, they are harassing their fellow Christians for not being the right sort of Christian. It is a sad, pathetic approach to belief if you ask me, which you did because you are reading my book.

---

[3] http://ucdata.berkeley.edu/rsfcensus/papers/Hout_FischerASA.pdf

Whatever you believe or don't believe is fine. Don't allow people who are so insecure in their faith bother you. Own who you are. If they throw a religious slur at you, own it. Say – thank you for that information, it's really helpful, and move on. If you aren't fun to hassle and you don't get upset or flustered at their taunts they will lose interest and try to find another target.

If you find that you are the target of proselytizing by well-intentioned individuals; the best way to get them to leave you alone is to make a deal with them, you will listen to them and read their literature if they will listen to you and read the literature you give to them. If they aren't willing to reciprocate, tell them to take a hike.

## Interfaith Volunteering

If religious tensions at your school are high because of religious bullying, the best way to solve that is to start an interfaith volunteer group. Encourage the 75% of your fellow students who are OK with religious freedom to stand up and be counted. You will not only do some good through your volunteering, you will also make any sort of religious bullying at your school uncool. Just remember to include the non-religious students as well, because they are often the targets of the worst of this sort of bullying.

### *Sexual Bullying*

One of the other areas of bullying that requires special attention is sexual bullying. Sexual identity is one of the most central aspects of our personality. To have that challenged can be very upsetting especially if your gender or sexual identity does not fit into someone else's idea of what is acceptable.

Attempts to stigmatize someone based on their sexual or gender identity is simply another attempt to control you through fear and intimidation. The more secure you are about who you are, the less bullies will be able to intimidate you and the less interesting you will be to them as a target.

In case you don't already know this, whoever you are and however you are as a person and as a sexual being is fine. That is who you are. The only thing you shouldn't be doing is bullying others about it and demanding that everyone else conform to your beliefs about how people should be. What is right for one person is not right for everyone else.

When it comes to gender, gender identity, sexual identity and sexual orientation, we humans are all over the map. There is no typical male and no typical female and in some cases these gender terms don't even apply. Attempting to conform to what you think is typical for your gender, whatever that is, is kind of pointless.

For the record, there are six types of chromosomal genders (xx, xo, xy, xxx, xxy, xyy). Our genitals (private parts) come in a wide variety of types, shapes, sizes and colors. Some people's genitals don't match what is typical for their chromosomal gender. In plain English this means that sometimes girls are born with penises and sometimes boys are born with vaginas. While this doesn't happen very often, it is a natural variation of the human body. Ultimately, however you are, is who you are and you should never be ashamed of who you are.

What you don't want to do is to try and be a perfect boy or a perfect girl. Perfect people don't exist. Trying to be perfect will drive you nuts. So don't go there. Besides, some of the top models in the world today are actually transgendered, which means they are both boy and girl at the same time. If they can be respected for who they are, you being who you are should be no problem at all. It really isn't that big of a deal anymore and people who make it a big deal are just showing you how insecure they are about their own sexuality.

## Another Way to Think About This

To give you an idea of exactly why you are OK just the way you are, consider the leaves on a tree. If you were to gather up a bunch of leaves that have fallen off a tree and put them side by side, you will see that none of the leaves are the same. They are all different. Some are bigger than others and some are smaller. Some bend in a funny way. I once found a leaf that seemed to grow in three directions at once. My son, who was six at the time, was concerned that this funny looking leaf was going to get teased by the other leaves for being so different. We decided to put the "funny" looking leaf side by side with the other leaves. Upon looking at our leaf collection, it became clear. There was no one correct way to be a leaf. All the leaves were different, but they were all fine looking leaves. They all had interesting things about them that made them slightly different from all the other leaves. Both my son and I agreed that the one we liked the best was the funny-looking one. We liked it because it was the most interesting leaf of all.

Yes, being different from everyone else can be difficult. It means you are easier to notice. However, being noticed is not always a bad thing. If your gender is atypical or even if it isn't, the first step to immunizing yourself against sexual bullying is to accept that who you are and how you are is fine. You are just like a leaf on a tree, unique.

It is also normal to be insecure about your gender and sexual identity. There isn't a human alive who hasn't dealt with wondering if they are normal. Most people are able to come to terms with their insecurities and eventually come to accept who they are and how they are.

The problem is that for some people their insecurities about whether or not they are normal are so bad that when they meet someone who doesn't conform to what they think is normal, it freaks them out and they don't know how to deal with it. It would be nice if people weren't such idiots.

Regardless, what they want is for you to stress yourself out trying to attain an impossible ideal of what they think the perfect person is. This is a fool's errand. It can't be done so don't even try. Know that these gender-obsessed bullies are idiots who are so insecure with themselves that they can't help but hassle others. Know this and you will feel much less intimidated by their idiocy. You may even feel sorry for them.

## Sexual Orientation

This brings us to the topic of sexual orientation. In addition to the pressure to conform to arbitrary gender roles, there is also pressure to be sexually interested in the "right" sort of person. In general, this means that boys are supposed to like girls and girls are supposed to like boys. The problem is our preference for who we like doesn't always conform to those expectations.

If you find yourself attracted to members of the same sex as yourself, don't worry. It happens fairly often and it is perfectly normal. If you find that you like both boys and girls, that is also normal. Study after study has shown that who you like and are attracted to is largely a product of your genes. Whichever gender you prefer, your preference is probably innate. This means that if you have a strong sexual orientation one way or the other, you were born that way. There is nothing wrong with you at all and your desire for sex is healthy.

More importantly, your sexual desires, whatever they are, are not something that you should worry about or try to change. Same-sex attractions, behaviors, and orientations are normal variants of human sexuality.

The only harm that results from these desires is the social and religious stigmas that are attached to them. The way to combat those stigmas is to understand that there is nothing wrong with you at all.

How do I know this? Well, it turns out that there have been LOTS of studies done on human sexuality and its variants: heterosexuality (preference for opposite sex), homosexuality (preference for same sex), bisexuality (preference for both sexes) and asexuality (lack of sexual attraction at all).

According to these studies, it turns out that it is rare to find someone who isn't, at some point, attracted to members of the same sex. Studies done in the 1950s by Kinsey showed that 46% of males respond sexually to both genders and that 37% of men have had sex with another man.

While most people's sexual orientation is fixed at birth and remain constant throughout their lives, for some people their preferences may change over time, though most people whose preferences are fluid tend to be girls. The point is, don't worry too much about who you find attractive, just enjoy the fact that you find someone attractive.

## Fighting Stigma

Why did I bother telling you all this? Well, despite the fact that sexual attraction is considered, by most people, to be healthy human behavior, there are still plenty of idiots out there who are afraid of sex. As we discussed before, they want you to be afraid of it too. Just like all bullies, they put a lot of effort into making you feel as afraid about sex as they are.

As I've said before, when someone harasses you about something, it is because their own fears are more than they can handle. Don't make their problem your problem. When it comes to sex, your desire for it is healthy. Everyone thinks about sex. If someone bullies you about sex, feel sorry for them. They are the ones with the problems.

I say this because studies have shown that thinking about sex and wanting sex is healthy for your mind and your body. Thinking that sex is bad or deviant or evil, on the other hand, causes a host of mental health problems. People who bully you about your sexual orientation and desires are doing so because they are suffering from a mental health problem. It doesn't matter how much they talk about morality to rationalize their fears, this is about their inability to cope with their insecurities and desires. Feel sorry for them, but don't join them in their misery.

This is especially important if you are being pressured to change your orientation. There are some religious beliefs that consider same-sex preference a defect and something that should be changed. This is one of the most dangerous ideas about sexuality in America today!

First, there is no evidence that your sexual orientation is harmful. But there is lots of evidence that trying to change your preference does a great deal of emotional harm. I know people who have been through sexual conversion programs and they all report the same thing. It didn't work. They were made to feel like a failure because it didn't work. They are still carrying around a great deal of emotional pain about the experience. Do not allow religious bigots to bully you into thinking there is something wrong with you. There isn't. It doesn't matter what you do, who you like is who you like.

65

Don't give in to the bullies on this. If you only ever stand up for one thing in your life, make it this. Attempting to change your sexual orientation would be a lot like trying to change your skin color by thinking different thoughts. It is not going to happen. Any attempt to control your thoughts is going to result in failure. Don't put yourself through that. There is a reason why <u>NO</u> major mental health organization approves of efforts to change sexual orientation and why ALL of them have policies stating such efforts cause harm.

## Cultural Perspective

If you live in the United States, you live in a culture that is slowly coming to terms with homosexuality. For a long time homosexuality was stigmatized. Much of that stigma has yet to go away. Don't let the fact that not everyone is enlightened bother you. Don't allow bullies to tell you that the way you are just isn't right. They don't have history on their side. According to Wikipedia there is a long history of cultures not only accepting homosexuality as no big deal, but of embracing transgendered individuals (or people whose gender defies stereotype) as people who have special powers. It is really just a western religious perspective that stigmatizes homosexuality. The good news is that the tides on that front are changing.

## What You Need to Know

When it comes to gay bashing, the people who are the most anti-gay are often the ones who are gay themselves and just don't want anyone to know. The number of politicians who were anti-gay but turned out to be gay would astound you.

Remember what I said at the beginning that most bullying is a way for bullies to draw attention away from themselves onto someone else who is more obviously vulnerable than they are? Well, this is the number one reason people bash gays and transgendered people. They figure if they are seen to be attacking gays, no one will accuse them of being gay themselves. People who gay bash are really just showing how insecure they are about their own sexuality.

This brings us back to the reason why bullies bully. People who gay bash are often in an incredible amount of emotional pain. They try to hide their desires and fears from everyone else. In short, they are miserable people. Feel sorry for them and don't take their negativity personally. Remember, it isn't actually about you. You aren't doing anything wrong. The problem lies entirely with them. They are afraid and they are struggling with their feelings. On top of it all, they probably don't have a family that is supportive of them and that just makes everything harder to deal with.

The reason this is important for you to know, is because in order to inoculate yourself from these sorts of bullies, you need to feel compassion for them. Feeling compassion doesn't excuse their behavior. It is about inoculating yourself against the negative emotions they are throwing at you. Instead of feeling fear and anger, you will feel compassion and sorrow for them, which is infinitely better. It won't help the bullies. But it will help you.

### Professional Help

Seek help if you find that your emotions are getting the better of you and that you are terrified of pretty much everyone. If you have good days where you feel pretty strong, and others, where you are just falling apart, you also need to seek help. Most importantly, if you are considering suicide, seek professional help immediately. You can find suicide hotlines online or at: http://www.suicidepreventionlifeline.org/

If you are thinking about suicide, don't just call a hotline. They can only help you in a moment of crisis. You need to find a local therapist who can work with you one on one over a period of time to help teach you the coping skills you need to learn. Most therapists work on a sliding scale, so don't allow your financial situation to stop you from seeking help. If all else fails, your county should have a mental health program you can use. Don't make excuses as to why you aren't seeking professional help. Just go get help. You will be glad you did.

Being bullied is a lot like being stalked and thoughts of suicide are not all that uncommon. It is very easy to lose hope when the bullying just keeps going on and on and on. Sometimes it doesn't seem like there will ever be light at the end of the tunnel. I know. I've been there. I've been stalked. I know how it feels to be utterly devoid of hope. I know what it is like to think that death might be a relief.

My advice to you is don't! Seek professional help. It really can help you get your life back. I am living proof of that. You just have to make a commitment to yourself. And that commitment is to continue living, just not like you have been.

People considering suicide often ask "why not die?" That is the wrong question to ask. It does not have a good answer. The question you should be asking is "why not live despite it all? It's a defiant question. When answered with a yes, it will give you the motivation to live, despite it all.

The next commitment you need to make is to no longer live in the hell you've been living in. One of my favorite quotes is, "If you are going through hell, keep going." Winston Churchill said that. To get through your personal hell, you are going to need professional help. If you could have done it on your own, you would not have considered suicide. Don't worry about the prospect of medication. Most of what a therapist does is help you learn very practical life skills that will help you cope better with the stress you are under. These can include things as simple as breathing exercises and yes, they really do help. Again, I am living proof that.

When I was being stalked, I was so nervous I was having panic attacks. I was having trouble even getting out of my house. I realized I was not coping well on my own so I went to a therapist for help. She taught me breathing techniques that helped interrupt my panic attacks before they got started. And yes, it really did work. Through journaling, I was able to identify what was triggering my panic. Within three months, I was panic attack free . I reclaimed my life and have never looked back. No drugs needed. My only regret is that I waited so long before I sought professional help.

I suffered for three years. I could barely get myself out of bed in the morning, let alone out of the house to go to work. If this describes you, you need to admit, that no, you are not coping well on your own. You need someone who can help you learn how to cope better. There is no shame in needing this sort of help. It is specialized help and you can't be expected to know how to do some of these things without being taught them. Not only did I get my life back, I was also able to truly ignore my stalker to the point I didn't even notice when he stopped harassing me. To me, that's nothing short of a miracle.

The hardest part of getting the help is admitting you need help. It is one of the hardest things you will ever do. But it is worth it because the relief you will feel of not having to pretend you are coping alright on your own when you clearly are not is immense. Go and seek a professional's help. You will be glad you did.

# On Becoming Fearless

*"Courage is resistance to fear, mastery of fear, not absence of fear."*

- Mark Twain

To be fearless is to be free from fear. But that's not really how it works. People who are fearless have fears; they just don't allow their fears to dictate their behavior. The actor Christian Bale once said, "I tend to think you're fearless when you recognize why you should be scared of things, but do them anyway."

No one is born fearless. The way to become fearless is to just decide that you aren't going to let your fears control you. The way you do that is to decide you aren't going to let your fears control you anymore.

Don't get me wrong. There are some things you should be afraid of, like jumping off a cliff for instance. However, most things we are afraid of have to do with what we think other people might think of us. While that matters too, we shouldn't let these fears prevent us from doing the things we like.

The problem with fear is that fear feels the same whether you are contemplating jumping off a cliff or singing for the first time in front of an audience. Your whole body responds the same way to both.

The way to conquer your fears is to figure out whether your fears are justified or not. You feel fear for a reason. It is an emotion designed to keep us from doing stupid things like jumping off a cliff. That sort of fear is a good thing. The problem is that it can also stop us from doing the things we really should be doing, like speaking in front of classmates. So, how do you tell your brain to relax when you are not in mortal danger?

Whenever I am afraid of something, I ask myself, what is the worst that could happen? If the worst that could happen does not involve physical injury or death to myself or another person, that tells me something. It tells me that my fears are about emotional danger not physical danger. Again,

71

this is good information to know because if it turns out that I am in physical danger, then I need to take my fears seriously.

However, if it turns out my fears are not of a physical nature, I need to decide whether or not my emotional fears are valid or not. As far as I am concerned, as long as what I want to do won't hurt another person, which is something I would never do on purpose, I figure I should probably just go ahead and do that thing I am afraid to do. After all, what's the worst that could happen? Sure, I could embarrass myself, but I can survive that.

After all, I've embarrassed myself hundreds of times and survived. I mean, who hasn't accidentally pee'd in their pants, or snorted while laughing or farted at an inappropriate time? We all have. We survive these experiences because we have no choice.

Regardless, by choosing to confront and face my fears and by doing those things I've been most afraid of, I conquered my fears and became fearless. There is no other way to become fearless, but to do the things you are afraid to do. As long as no permanent physical damage is done, you will survive. Think of it this way: if you embarrass yourself, you will have a great story to tell your grandkids one day about how stupid you were when you were a kid. Those stories are priceless.

The good news is that the more you practice being fearless, the easier it becomes. People who are fearless teach themselves how to be fearless because they have, at some point, decided that they don't want to live in fear anymore. It is a choice. It doesn't mean you won't be afraid or that everything is going to be wonderful and everyone will treat you well or that you won't do incredibly stupid things for people to laugh at. You will do stupid things and people will laugh at you.

Instead, what being fearless means is that, despite your fears, you are going to be the person you want to be and that you are going to do the things you want to do and more importantly, you are going to do the things that you need to do. Most importantly, being fearless means you won't let anyone else bully you into hiding your true self from others.

### *Harnessing Your True Power*

There is a reason why every single adult you meet tells you the same thing. Be yourself and stop worrying about what other people think. The reason we keep telling you this is because, this really is the only way to be happy. We've been where you are and we learned the hard way. Trying not to be dorky doesn't work and no matter how hard you try, the bullies are still going to tease you anyway. You might as well do the things that make you happy and to heck with what the bullies think.

Yes, it does take courage to not care what other people think. Yes, it is hard to endure being teased because you are doing something incredibly dorky. What you don't realize is that only a few people are laughing at you. Those few people are the bullies. They are teasing you and bullying you because they are jealous of you. They are too afraid to be themselves and they want you to be afraid too.

What everyone else is thinking is just how darned cool you are. Most people, even if they think you are a bit weird and silly, will be in awe of you when you do something intentionally dorky. Lady Gaga does incredibly dorky things. That's why she's admired. Anyone who isn't a bully will wish they had your courage every single time you decide not to let your fears rule you. That's a LOT of power and respect when you think of it.

I realize that you probably don't believe me right now. You are probably thinking, yeah right, I will be teased if I wear the wrong clothes or read the wrong book or see the wrong movies or hang out with the wrong people. But do me a favor. Just try it once and see what happens.

Once you try it you will find out, yeah – the bullies responded exactly as you expected, and you know what – it wasn't that bad.


## Multi-Colored Striped Socks

How dorky am I talking about? Well, how about wearing knee-high multicolored striped socks with shorts and sandals, which I did once in high school. The way I figure it, if you are going to be dorky, be really dorky,

Yes, people laughed at me. Heck, I laughed at me. I thought I looked ridiculous and I did. That was why I did it. The point is that people, including the popular kids, were in awe of me for being so courageous to go against fashion in such an out there way. How do I know? Well, as I said, I did the multicolored sock thing as a joke, just to be dorky and funny. So imagine my surprise the following week when several of the popular girls showed up in multicolored striped socks! Not only did I survive my over the top attempt at dorkiness, I started a fashion trend. True story.

The more you own your behavior and your mistakes and your dorkiness, the less impact a bully's teasing and taunting will have on you and the more respect you will receive from everyone else.

More importantly, you don't need to worry about being socially ostracized because of your dorkiness. As long as you own the fact that you are a dork, you will find that people will want to be your friend. That's because people are drawn to the fearless. Dorky creative kids will want to hang out with you because: a) there's safety in numbers and; b) you showed them it was OK to be as dorky as they really are. That's something to be proud of.

I was openly dorky in middle school and high school. I had a deformed jaw. Yet, I never lacked friends, I was never bullied and I was considered a leader by my fellow students. I am living proof this really does work.

### One Final Lesson
No one wants to live in fear of bullies or other obnoxious people. To inoculate yourself against bullies and other obnoxious people you need to:

1) Know what makes a bully tick and how bullying happens. Knowledge is power.

2) Be prepared. Have a plan for how you want to handle bullying before you get bullied. What will you do if you are a target? What if one of your friends is being bullied? Have a plan, be prepared.

3) Find a way to feel compassion for bullies. There is nothing they hate more than being pitied. But more important than that, feeling sorry

for them helps you. It is really hard to be upset, when all you can think about is just how pathetic and miserable a bully really is.

4) Always remember, you can train a bully to stop. Don't give them the reward they want. Respond in the most boring way possible and they will eventually get bored with you.

5) Know when to ask for help. If a bully isn't just being obnoxious but is threatening or harming someone, it needs to be reported.

6) Love yourself. If you love and like yourself the way you are, there is nothing a bully can say that will hurt you. Always remember, you are fine just the way you are.

7) Get help if you need it. Don't be afraid to ask for help if your emotions are getting the best of you. There are professionals that can help teach you new coping skills that really will help.

8) Be fearless. The more you trust in yourself, the happier you are going to be. Bullies learn very quickly to avoid confident people, because confident/happy people are bully proof. Their fearlessness acts as a vaccine that keeps the bullies away.

All it takes is for you to decide that you are going to be fearless. And you will be. Is it hard? Yes. Do we all get bogged down by our fears? Yes. Can our fears immobilize us? Yes, they frequently do. So what!

Being fearless doesn't mean being perfect. It just means that you are at least conscious of your fears and you are trying to prevent them from controlling your life. It means that you aren't going to let bullies bully you. Not only are you going to stand up for yourself, you are going to make it your responsibility to stand up for your classmates as well.

Every time you choose to do the right thing, every time you choose to do something that makes you happy, even though you know other people might laugh or find it strange, you gain more courage and you become more fearless. The choice to be fearless becomes easier and easier.

No one is born fearless. They become fearless by refusing to live in fear anymore. Once you decide to not live in fear, the rest becomes easier.

*"We gain strength, and courage, and confidence by each experience in which we really stop to look fear in the face... we must do that which we think we cannot."*

        - Eleanor Roosevelt

# About the Author

Jennifer Hancock is a writer, speaker and Humanist.

She can be found on the web at
http://www.jen-hancock.com/

Her other books include:
*The Humanist Approach to Happiness: Practical Wisdom*
and
*Jennifer Hancock's Handy Humanism Handbook.*

(Note: The Handy Humanism Handbook is available as a free e-book if you sign up for Jen's mailing list at the website listed above)

If you are interested in learning how to think more effectively about ethics and decision making as well as how to cope better in your life overall, check out Jen's 6 week *Humanist Life Skills Course: Living Made Simpler* available online at http://humanisthappiness.com

Jennifer has a variety of other online resource and training materials available at her website including a podcast, blog and more.

She is also available to do trainings and workshops on this material.

~~~~~~

**Connect with her online:**
Twitter: http://twitter.com/#!/JentheHumanist
Facebook: http://www.facebook.com/JentheHumanist
Or sign up for her mailing list: http://eepurl.com/c3LuI and get a free e-book

To download bullying documentation sheets and a how to help your child tip sheet, visit the book's website at: http://thebullyvaccine.com

Made in the USA
Monee, IL
17 April 2023

32005405R00049